The Ultimate Self-Regulation Book For Kids Ages 8-12

The Complete Guide to Mindfulness, Emotional Intelligence, and Self-Control

BEN STEVENSON

Contents

1. UNDERSTANDING SELF-REGULATION 9

2. BUILDING SELF-AWARENESS 17

3. CULTIVATING SELF-CONTROL 27

4. SELF-REGULATION FOR ACADEMIC SUCCESS 38

5. SOCIAL-EMOTIONAL LEARNING FOR SELF-REGULATION 49

6. SUSTAINING SELF-REGULATION: REFLECTION AND RESOURCES 60

PREFACE

The society we live in is always shifting and moving at a rapid pace; thus, it is more necessary than ever before to teach children how to exercise self-control. The purpose of this comprehensive handbook is to equip children between the ages of 8 and 12 with the resources they require to manage their emotions, thoughts, and behaviors in a healthy manner, so developing grit and increasing their level of self-control.

Within the first chapter, "Understanding Self-Regulation," the concept of self-regulation is discussed, along with the significance of this skill for children. We are going to discuss what self-regulation is, why it is so important, and all of the wonderful things that it can do for you. It is possible for children to become more motivated to acquire these essential abilities if they are aware of the significance of self-regulation and how it may be applied to their own life.

awareness: Chapter 2 of The Foundation of Self-Regulation discusses the fundamental principles of awareness as a practice. Concentrating on the here and now without passing judgment on it is what it means to be mindful. By experimenting with a variety of mindfulness practices, children can develop a greater awareness of their thoughts, feelings, and overall sensations. Self-regulation is the initial step toward self-regulation, which offers children the ability to respond to circumstances rather than responding without thinking about what they had experienced.

Developing Emotional Intelligence is the topic of discussion in Chapter 3, which focuses on the most significant aspect of emotional intelligence. Teenagers and children will acquire the skills necessary to identify and comprehend their own feelings, as well as the skills necessary to deal with events that cause them to experience emotions. Through the development of their emotional intelligence, children are able to deal with challenging situations, acquire the ability to care about others, and form meaningful friendships.

The fourth chapter, titled "Self-Control Techniques," discusses self-control and the methods that can be used to inhibit urges. Children are going to acquire helpful advice and strategies for enhancing their capacity for self-control with the assistance of this chapter. By acquiring skills like as postponing gratification and exercising self-control over their impulses, children will acquire the ability to make intelligent choices and prevent themselves from acting without first giving them some thought.

In the fifth chapter, titled "Building Resilience," children are taught how to be resilient in the face of adversity. They will learn how to adopt a growth mindset, how to view challenges as opportunities to learn and grow, and how to get back on their feet after experiencing failure. By cultivating their resilience, children can acquire the self-assurance and resolve that they require in order to successfully navigate the challenges that they face throughout their life.

As they progress through Chapter 6: Practicing Self-Regulation in Everyday Life, children will acquire skills that can be applied to a variety of aspects of their lives. Throughout their lives, children will acquire valuable skills that will assist them in maintaining their self-control and mental health in a range of contexts, including at home, at school, and with their friends.

When it comes to controlling your emotions in general, patterns and healthy habits can be of great assistance. This topic is discussed in Chapter 7, "Creating Healthy Habits." By participating in this exercise, children will gain an understanding of the significance of maintaining consistent routines, developing positive habits, and being aware of the significance of sleep and food for their overall health.

In Chapter 8, "Overcoming Challenges," children are provided with the resources they require to deal with everyday issues such as stress, arguments, and the pressures of being in a group. Children can demonstrate poise and resiliency in the face of challenging circumstances if they are taught how to manage stress and anger, how to resolve arguments in a peaceful manner, and how to avoid being influenced by negative people.

Creating a positive image of yourself and learning to treat yourself with kindness are the two most important aspects of boosting your self-esteem, as discussed in Chapter 9. Learning about self-esteem, how to boost their self-worth, and how to be kind to themselves are all topics that will be covered in this lesson. They will be better able to accept their individual characteristics and develop a healthy sense of who they are as a result of this.

There is a strong emphasis placed on self-care in Chapter 10: Maintaining Well-Being. This chapter discusses a variety of topics, including self-care routines, strategies for dealing with bullying, and the development of positive connections. By prioritizing their own self-care, children can maintain control of their emotional well-being and establish reasonable boundaries for the ways in which they interact with other people.

In addition, the purpose of "The Ultimate Self-Regulation Book For Kids Ages 8-12: The Complete Guide to Mindfulness, Emotional Intelligence, and Self-Control" is to provide children with the knowledge and resources they require in order to acquire essential skills for self-regulation. It is through reading this book that children will acquire valuable skills that will help them better manage their emotions, become more self-aware, enhance their capacity for self-control, become more resilient, and improve their overall health. In the event that children acquire these vital abilities, they will be better equipped to deal with the highs and lows that come with being a child and will develop into self-assured and self-aware individuals. Let's embark on this path of change together, providing children with the resources they require to take responsibility for their own emotions and actions.

1

Understanding Self-Regulation

The ability to self-regulate is an essential skill that enables children to effectively manage their cognitive processes, emotional states, and behaviors. In the process of cultivating emotional intelligence, mindfulness, and self-control, it acts as the basic pillar. In this chapter, we will discuss the notion of self-regulation, as well as its significance in the lives of children and the numerous advantages that it can provide.

"What exactly is self-regulation?"

The capacity to monitor and exert control over one's own thoughts, feelings, and actions is what is meant by the term "self-regulation." It entails being conscious of our internal states, being able to recognize the factors that bring about those states, and being able to react in a manner that is both healthy and acceptable. When children are able to self-regulate, they are more ready to deal with difficult circumstances, to make decisions that require careful consideration, and to maintain good relationships with both themselves and with other people.

The Reasons Why Self-Regulation Is So Important

The ability to self-regulate is very important in many different parts of a child's life. Their entire well-being, as well as their academic performance and social interactions, are all greatly impacted as a result. When children are able to self-regulate, they are better able to maintain their concentration, deal with interruptions, and participate actively in their education. Consequently, they are able to exercise control over impulsive behaviors, adhere to directions, and finish work in a more effective manner. Additionally, children that are able to self-regulate tend to demonstrate higher self-control, which leads to fewer behavioral issues and disruptions within the household.

It is also very important to note that self-regulation has a significant impact on the social life of a child. Children are better able to navigate social settings, resolve disagreements in a calm manner, and effectively communicate their needs when they are able to regulate their emotions and behaviors (also known as emotional regulation). Through the development of this skill, they are able to cultivate healthy relationships, sympathize with other people, and establish a sense of connectedness among their peer group.

What are the Advantages of Self-Regulation?

The benefits of self-regulation extend well beyond the circumstances that are currently occurring. There is a correlation between children who have excellent self-regulation abilities and higher academic accomplishment, improved self-confidence, and a greater sense of well-being within themselves. It is possible for youngsters to approach their education with better concentration and perseverance if they are able to control their feelings and urges. They have the ability to cope with stress and pressure, which enables them to do better on tests and evaluations.

In addition, children who are able to self-regulate are better equipped to deal with problems and difficulties that they may encounter throughout their lives. They cultivate resilience, which is the capacity to recover quickly from failures and to endure in the face of challenges while overcoming obstacles. Children that have the ability to self-regulate are better able to adjust to new situations, are better prepared to deal with stressful situations, and exhibit greater emotional stability. The acquisition of these abilities contributes to the general mental health and well-being of the individual, resulting in a life that is both happier and more rewarding.

Gaining an Understanding of the Process of Self-Regulation

To have a complete understanding of self-regulation, it is essential to realize that it is a process that occurs in a sequential order. To begin, self-awareness serves as the cornerstone around which self-regulation is built. When it comes to their feelings, ideas, and physical experiences, children need to be able to identify and comprehend them. Through the cultivation of this awareness, children are able to precisely identify their emotional states and comprehend the factors that are directly responsible for them.

The second benefit of self-monitoring is that it gives youngsters the opportunity to see how they behave in response to various circumstances.

Being aware of one's own thoughts and actions, as well as the influence those things have on oneself and others, is a necessary component of it. Children have the ability to become aware of any patterns, triggers, or events that have a tendency to generate particular feelings or reactions when they engage in self-monitoring.

Children are able to progress to the next step, which is the most important component of self-control, once they have achieved self-awareness and have exercised self-monitoring. The ability to control one's impulses, to postpone satisfaction, and to make deliberate decisions rather than giving in to one's immediate urges are all components of self-control. Children are better able to think before they act, explore several options, and make choices that are in line with their long-term objectives as a result of this.

Exercise, perseverance, and ongoing growth are all necessary components in the process of developing self-regulation. Through the development of these skills, children are able to become more adept at self-regulating their feelings, thoughts, and behaviors, which ultimately results in an improvement in their general functioning and mental health.

We will investigate a variety of approaches and methods during the course of this book in order to assist youngsters in the development and improvement of their abilities to self-regulate. It is possible for children to gradually improve their ability to properly regulate their emotions, thoughts, and behaviors if they actively participate in exercises, practice the concepts that are offered, and incorporate self-regulation into their daily lives.

In addition, it is essential to keep in mind that the process of self-regulation is a journey that lasts a lifetime, and that children will continue to hone and improve these skills as they mature. It is possible for children to establish a solid foundation for self-regulation so that they are better prepared for success in both their personal and academic life. This can be accomplished by beginning early and providing children with the tools and support they need.

Therefore, let us go on this revolutionary journey together, as we assist youngsters in developing the ability to self-regulate, cultivate mindfulness, develop emotional intelligence, and exercise self-control. Children will be able to realize their full potential, thrive in a world that is always changing, and cultivate a sense of inner peace and well-being if they incorporate these skills into their everyday life. Get ready to explore the countless opportunities that are waiting for you in the future!

2

Building Self-Awareness

The process of developing our capacity for self-regulation is a process that begins with the development of self-awareness, which is a vital beginning step towards the development of our capacity. Before we can make progress toward achieving self-awareness, we must first recognize and acknowledge the feelings, beliefs, and patterns of behavior that we have internally. The ability to have a more profound grasp of themselves, their triggers, and the responses they have to those stimuli is provided to children as a result of this. Developing children's self-awareness and establishing the groundwork for the development of skills that will enable them to self-regulate will be the topic of discussion in the following chapter.

We will go over a range of ways and activities that can help children develop these skills.

The Power to Transform That Mindfulness Gives

Mindfulness is a great method that can assist children in becoming more self-aware. These youngsters can benefit from the practice of mindfulness. It is necessary to pay attention to the here and now without casting judgment on it and with full awareness in order to put it into practice. via the cultivation of a more profound understanding of their internal experiences, including their thoughts, feelings, and the sensations that occur within their bodies, children have the capacity to build a more profound awareness of it via the practice of mindfulness.

It is easy to begin educating children about mindfulness by beginning with something that is quite simple, such as practicing mindful breathing. Encourage children to focus their attention on their breathing and provide them with the opportunity to become conscious of the sensation of air entering and leaving their bodies. It is possible for children to direct their focus to their breathing and to firmly establish themselves in the here and now in order to bring their attention to the physiological sensations that they are experiencing and to find a sense of grounding in the current moment.

There are many different types of mindfulness, one of which is the practice of aware observation. The act of examining an object in great detail, paying attention to its color, texture, shape, and any other characteristics that may be present, should be encouraged for children. When children are encouraged to use their senses to the fullest extent possible, they are able to develop a greater capacity to appropriately perceive and explain their experiences, as well as a greater capacity to become more attentive to the current moment.

A consciousness of one's own emotions

When it comes to growing one's self-awareness, one of the most important components is the ability to recognize and interpret one's own sensations. Helping children develop emotional awareness enables them to understand and describe their feelings in an effective manner. This capacity is a significant benefit of providing assistance to youngsters. In order to have emotional awareness, one must be able to detect a variety of feelings, know the elements that lead to those feelings, and be able to appropriately label and communicate those sentiments.

In order to increase the level of emotional awareness that children have, it is important to involve them in activities that provide them the opportunity to analyze and discuss their feelings. It would be beneficial if you could supply them with a feelings chart or emotions wheel, which depicts a variety of feelings and can serve as a point of reference for recognizing and categorizing emotions. This would be of great assistance to them. When it comes to the various emotions and the triggers that are associated with them, it is important to foster conversations that are open and devoid of judgment.

Furthermore, storytelling is a powerful tool that can assist children in recognizing and comprehending the variety of feelings that they experience. This is because storytelling is a powerful technique. Take use of novels that are appropriate for the particular age group, or compose stories that depict individuals going through a variety of emotions. Children should be encouraged to think about the feelings that the characters could be experiencing after they have done reading or listening to the story. They should also be encouraged to think about the events or circumstances that led to those sentiments. Through regular practice of this activity, one can improve their capacity for empathy as well as their emotional understanding.

A Method of Reflection as a Practice

The promotion of children's self-awareness includes a number of different components, one of which is the assistance of encouraging children to participate in reflective practices. Children have the opportunity to consider their experiences, decisions, and reactions through the process of reflection, which ultimately results in a more profound understanding of who they are as individuals. Children are able to recognize patterns, recognize triggers, and acquire insight into their thoughts and behaviors when they engage in the practice of reflecting on their experiences.

Writing in a journal is an effective way to engage in introspection since it promotes reflection. It is essential to enable children to freely express their thoughts, feelings, and experiences by providing them with a diary or notepad in which they can write down their thoughts. By encouraging children to reflect on their day, analyze challenging circumstances, and convey their feelings in an open and honest manner, it is crucial to support their development. Children and adolescents are better able to cultivate a feeling of self-awareness and participate in self-reflection when they maintain a journaling practice on a regular basis.

Participating in guided self-questioning is yet another type of reflective practice that can be utilized. When children have been through significant experiences or interactions, it is essential to encourage them to ask themselves questions that require them to reflect on their previous experiences. Here are some examples of questions that can be used for the purpose of engaging in self-reflection: In that particular circumstance, how did I feel throughout that time? Can you tell me about the circumstances that lead to those feelings? What I need to know is how I responded, and whether or not it was successful. In the event that I were to repeat the process, what would I do differently? Children are encouraged to think about different ways of approaching or solving difficulties when they are engaged in the process of guided self-questioning. This technique prompts children to reflect on their experiences and encourages them to think about it.

Facilitating Communication That Is Both Open And Honest

When it comes to the development of self-awareness, open communication is an essential component that must be present. It is essential to give children with a safe and supportive environment in which they are able to openly express their thoughts, feelings, and experiences without the fear of being punished for doing so. It is important that children be taught to engage in active listening, and that they be provided with the chance to talk about their experiences and feelings without the fear of being judged or ridiculed.

In order to encourage children to engage in self-reflection and introspection, it is important to have open talks with them on a regular basis. Ask them questions that have open-ended replies. While it is important to validate their experiences, it is also important to encourage children to talk about their ideas, thoughts, and feelings. When children engage in open discourse, they are able to develop a stronger awareness of their own thoughts, feelings, and behaviors, as well as an understanding of how these things affect both themselves and others. This is because adults are able to help kids comprehend how these things affect others.

When it comes to the process of gaining self-regulation, one of the most important steps is to cultivate one's own self-awareness. It is possible for children to acquire a more profound understanding of themselves through the cultivation of emotional awareness, the involvement in reflective activities, the promotion of open communication, and the adoption of mindfulness practices. This is something that can be accomplished. Children who have a greater awareness of themselves are better able to effectively manage their thoughts, feelings, and behaviors, which eventually results in higher self-regulation and general well-being. This is because children have a greater capacity to know themselves.

The importance of developing self-control is going to be examined in greater detail in the following chapter, which will be presented after this one. In order to equip young people with the ability to control their impulses, make judgments that are founded on serious deliberation, and effectively govern their behaviors, we will study a number of different strategies and techniques. This transformative path toward self-regulation is something that we ought to continue doing jointly in order to achieve our goals.

3

Cultivating Self-Control

A person's ability to exercise self-control is among the most essential aspects of self-regulation. Having the ability to control one's impulses, to resist temptations, and to make choices that are intentional and in accordance with one's goals and values is what is meant by the word "self-control." During the process of developing the ability to exert self-control, children acquire the capacity to effectively regulate their actions and to make decisions that are beneficial to them. Within the confines of this chapter, we will study a range of ways and strategies that can assist children in growing their capacity for self-control and improving their overall self-regulation abilities.

These are both areas that can be beneficial to the development of children.

How to Acquire Knowledge Regarding the Brain

In order to construct self-control in an appropriate manner, it is necessary to have a good grasp of the function of the brain in the process of behavior regulation. Decision-making, impulse control, and emotional regulation are all functions that are attributed to different regions of the brain. Several different regions of the brain are responsible for carrying out these duties. The prefrontal cortex, which is responsible for executive activities such as planning, problem-solving, and self-control, is one of the most essential regions in the brain. On the other hand, this region is not fully developed in children, which is the reason why they have a tendency to struggle with exercising self-control. This is because children's brains are still coming into their own.

Through the provision of children with an explanation of the development of the brain in words that are appropriate for their age, we may be able to assist them in realizing that self-control is a skill that can be gained over the course of time. Children should be encouraged to conceive of self-control as a muscle that can be enhanced through practice and effort. This is something that should be encouraged.

Cultivating Capabilities for Self-Control and Management

It is possible to enhance the development of self-control in children through the implementation of a range of strategies and procedures. Several different approaches are being utilized in order to enhance children's capacity to delay gratification, exercise self-control over impulses, and arrive at decisions after giving them some due consideration. Through the application of the following successful tactics, one can cultivate the ability to exercise self-control:

As part of the mindful pause, children should be instructed on the significance of pausing for reflection before acting on impulses. This is something that should be taught to them. Provide them with instructions to take a few deep breaths and consider a number of different ways in which they could react to the circumstance. In the course of this pause, children are provided with the opportunity to acquire clarity and choose a response that is in accordance with their overall goals and values.

2. Goal-Setting: Children should be assisted in the process of developing objectives that are specific and possible to achieve. By focusing their attention on specific goals, children can develop the self-control that is necessary for overcoming distractions and making progress toward their aims. This can be accomplished through the process of concentrating on specific targets. Ensure that your goals are broken down into smaller, more manageable activities if you want to

improve your motivation and achievement. This will help you reach your goals more effectively.

The third goal of distraction management is to teach children methods that will allow them to deal with situations that are either distracting or enticing. In the event that they are challenged with temptations, you should encourage them to redirect their attention to an activity that is either more productive or more gratifying. By way of illustration, a youngster can divert their attention away from the desire to snack on unhealthy foods by participating in a hobby that they enjoy or by engaging in physical activity rather than giving in to the temptation.

When it comes to assisting young people in better controlling their thoughts and emotions, it is essential to encourage them to engage in positive self-talk. Instructing youngsters to replace negative or impulsive notions with ones that are uplifting and empowering is a key step in the positive development of children. Children have the ability to learn how to better manage challenging situations, maintain their attention, and make decisions that are under their own control by engaging in self-talk.

Visualize Success: Parents should encourage their children to imagine themselves successfully avoiding temptations and choosing decisions that are under their own control. This is an important step in the process of achieving success. Children's inherent ability to imagine happy possibilities is increased through the practice of visualization, which also helps children feel more confidence in their ability to exercise self-control. Visualization is a technique that has been used for centuries.

It is crucial to build routines and rituals because structure and consistency are essential components of self-control. As a result, it is important to do this. Providing assistance to children in the establishment of routines and rituals is important in terms of assisting them in the development of self-control. The establishment of normal sleeping patterns, the participation in regular physical activity, and the allocation of specified time for studying or doing assignments are all ways to build an atmosphere that is conducive to the development of self-control.

Help youngsters develop the ability to delay gratification by having them participate in activities. The discipline of delaying gratification consists of seven steps, and this is the seventh one. Young children can learn the ability to exercise patience and self-control through activities such as playing board games that need them to take turns or participating in projects that take a long time. It is possible for kids to develop these skills through activities.

One of the most important things to bear in mind is that the process of developing self-control is a gradual one. Take this into consideration. In situations where children are confronted with challenges and setbacks, it is essential to urge them to persevere and to be patient with themselves.

Children are able to cultivate the self-assurance and resiliency that are necessary for the successful cultivation of self-control when they are acknowledged and celebrated for their advances. This allows children to better manage their own behavior.

Modeling and reinforcement (also known as modeling)

We, as adults, play a crucial part in the process of instructing children on how to exercise self-control and how to do it effectively. Through the manner in which we conduct ourselves, we are providing younger generations with a fantastic model to emulate. By continually demonstrating self-control in our own behaviors and decision-making, we are able to assist youngsters in understanding the value of this skill as well as the significant benefits it offers.

In addition to this, it is essential to offer youngsters with positive reinforcement and acknowledgement whenever they exhibit self-control. This not only motivates children to continue exercising self-control practices, but it also encourages them to continue efforts that they have been doing. A compliment is given to young people when they are praised for their capability to resist temptations, their patience, and their ability to make decisions. The use of verbal or tangible rewards is another method that can be implemented for the purpose of reinforcing the individuals' best efforts to develop self-control.

It is possible that incorporating activities that require self-control into one's daily routine could prove to be beneficial. Participating in mindfulness exercises as a family, developing goals that are shared by all members of the family, and practicing self-control techniques together are all examples of activities that can assist improve the ability of the entire family to regulate their own emotions and behaviors.

In a nutshell, one of the most important aspects of self-regulation is developing one's capacity to exert self-control. We are able to create self-control in children by first gaining an awareness of the function that the brain plays, then teaching thoughtful pauses, then defining objectives, then controlling distractions, then fostering positive self-talk, then picturing achievement, then establishing routines, then practicing delayed gratification, then modeling, and finally providing reward. The children who take part in these activities acquire the abilities that are necessary to properly regulate their impulses, to make decisions that are well thought out, and to effectively guide their behaviors.

During the course of the following chapter, we are going to look into the connection that exists between self-regulation and academic success. In this session, we are going to discuss a variety of strategies that can teach children how to apply their self-regulation skills in the context of their learning, which will ultimately lead to improved academic performance and overall growth. Let us move forward together on this road toward self-regulation, which will change our lives forever, are you ready?

4

Self-Regulation for Academic Success

Academic success is directly proportional to one's capacity for self-regulation, which is a vital component. It provides children with the ability to effectively manage their emotions, thoughts, and behaviors, which ultimately leads to increased concentration, organization, and motivation with regard to the instructional contexts in which they are instructed. The purpose of this chapter is to study a range of ways and methods that can help children put their self-regulation skills into practice, so improving their academic progress and general development. These approaches and methods can be found in this chapter.

In the context of educational institutions, the principle of self-regulation

It is possible to foster the development of self-regulation in children by doing so by providing them with a learning environment that is not just supportive but also structured. Within educational settings, it is essential to foster an environment that encourages self-regulation, and the following are some of the most important strategies:

1. Clearly Defined Expectations: When it comes to behavior and performance, it is also important to establish expectations that are not just explicit but also acceptable. In order to make certain that children are aware of what is expected of them, it is essential to be sure that these expectations are communicated to them in their entirety. This can be accomplished by utilizing either written

instructions or visual indicators in order to better define what is expected of you.

A significant component of the process of goal-setting is the instruction of young people in the skill of planning and establishing objectives for their academic work, both in the short term and in the long term. You should provide assistance to them in devising a strategy to fulfill the goals that we have established for them and in breaking down the responsibilities into smaller, more manageable portions. Using this strategy, which allows for the promotion of self-regulation, clarity and a road map for achievement are provided to the individual.

3. Time Management and Organization: Teach young people the skills necessary to manage their time effectively and to organize their information. Children should be encouraged to make use of tools such as planners, calendars, and checklists in order to keep track of their study schedules, assignments, and deadlines. It is crucial to

encourage children to use these tools at all times. Through the utilization of these strategies, young people are able to cultivate a sense of responsibility as well as the ability to effectively self-regulate their time.

4. Study Strategies: Assist young people in the process of establishing effective study strategies that will improve their learning and retention of information. The instruction of youngsters in a variety of strategies, including active reading, summarizing content, mnemonic devices, and self-quizzing, is of utmost importance. In order to enhance the process of self-regulation, these strategies stimulate active involvement and metacognition, which are both components of the process.

You should assist students in recognizing and managing disruptive variables that may be present in their educational contexts. This is the fifth and last step in the management of distractions. They should be instructed on strategies such as establishing a special location for studying, turning off electronic gadgets, and using headphones that drown out background noise. These are all methods that should be taught to them. It is possible for children to improve their ability to concentrate and self-regulate their attention by minimizing the number of distractions that they are exposed to.

When children are facing challenging academic assignments, it is essential to encourage them to participate in positive self-talk in order to help them cope with the challenges. The importance of teaching youngsters to replace self-defeating or negative thoughts with affirmations that are positive and supportive of them cannot be overstated. By creating resiliency, motivation, and a growth mentality, talking to oneself in a constructive manner helps to cultivate self-regulation. This is accomplished through the cultivation of self-talk.

Facilitating the Development of Capabilities for Self-Regulation

Furthermore, in addition to providing an atmosphere that is suitable to learning, we are able to support children in the development of self-regulation abilities, which are directly tied to the academic accomplishment of the children. The following is a list of tactics that have shown to be successful:

1. Emotional Regulation: When children are working on academic tasks or studying, it is important to teach them strategies that will enable them to have control over their moods. You should urge them to take short breaks, engage in exercises that include deep breathing, or engage in physical activity in order to alleviate tension. It is recommended that you do this. The ability to control one's feelings is associated with improvements in one's capacity to concentrate, resilience, and general well-being overall.

It is possible to assist youngsters in becoming more aware of their own thought processes by guiding them through the process of establishing metacognitive skills. This is referred to as metacognition. Children should be given instruction in techniques such as self-reflection, self-monitoring, and self-evaluation that they can use to improve themselves. It is possible for children to effectively self-regulate their learning when they have a firm understanding of the manner in which they learn most effectively, as well as when they are able to recognize their own strengths and areas in which they may improve.

3. Problem-Solving: When children are faced with academic challenges, it is essential to encourage them to utilize problem-solving strategies in order to overcome these challenges. Instructing kids on numerous strategies, such as breaking down problems into smaller sections, coming up with alternative solutions, and analyzing the usefulness of various methods, is something that you should accomplish. Individuals who have problem-solving skills are better able to self-regulate their behavior

because these skills encourage critical thinking and adaptation.

4. Encourage children to have a growth mentality, which is the idea that their skills and intelligence may be developed through the application of work and practice. Kids should be encouraged to have this mentality. It is important to instill in children the understanding that mistakes and challenges are opportunities for growth, and you should also encourage them to view their failures as opportunities for personal growth and development. Individuals are able to strengthen their capacity for self-regulation through the cultivation of a growth mindset, which fosters resiliency, motivation, and a determination to persevere in the face of success or failure.

5. Suggest to children that they engage in self-assessment and reflection in order to encourage them to regularly review their own progress and reflect on what they have learnt at regular intervals. In order to achieve this goal, it is

possible to provide them with opportunities for self-evaluation. For instance, you may encourage them to review their work or ask for feedback on how well they performed. Self-assessment and reflection are two behaviors that contribute to the development of self-regulation. These practices encourage self-awareness, accountability, and continual growth, which are all essential components of self-regulation.

There are specific requirements and preferences that are specific to each child, and it is vital to modify strategies and procedures in order to satisfy those specific requirements and preferences. Recognizing that the capacity to self-regulate is something that tends to develop over time and requires constant practice and guidance is something that should be acknowledged. To ensure that the children continue to grow and develop, it is important to recognize the accomplishments of the children and to provide them with feedback that is not only constructive but also encouraging.

Learning should include activities that encourage self-regulation, and these activities should be incorporated into the process. You may, for instance, begin a session with a brief mindfulness exercise, encourage students to keep a journal about their thoughts and the strategies they utilize when confronted with challenging tasks, or hold group discussions on themes relating to self-regulation approaches. Both of these activities are great ways to engage students in the learning process. By cultivating a culture of self-regulation and incorporating self-regulation activities into the curriculum, our objective is to cultivate abilities that will last a lifetime. This will be accomplished by incorporating self-regulation techniques into instruction.

The ability to self-regulate is an absolute requirement for the aim of achieving academic success. The development of self-regulation skills such as emotional regulation, metacognition, problem-solving, and a growth mindset are all ways in which we empower children to flourish academically and to embrace a love of learning that will last a lifetime. The creation of a learning environment that is supportive, the facilitation of goal-setting and planning, the teaching of skills related to organization and time management, the promotion of effective study strategies, the management of distractions, and the encouragement of positive self-talk are all ways in which we empower children to accomplish these things.

We are going to study the function that social-emotional learning plays in the process of establishing self-regulation in the following chapter. During this session, we will investigate many approaches that can be applied to enhance children's social awareness, relational abilities, and responsible decision-making, which will ultimately result in the development of comprehensive self-regulation. Should we continue together on this journey toward self-regulation and academic excellence, which has the potential to completely transform our lives?

5

Social-Emotional Learning for Self-Regulation

Children can be improved in their ability to self-regulate through the use of a powerful technique called social-emotional learning (SEL). The development of the skills and attitudes necessary for managing emotions, constructing meaningful relationships, and making responsible decisions is the primary focus of social and emotional learning (SEL). By incorporating social and emotional learning (SEL) into the lives of children, we can provide them the ability to properly regulate their behaviors, feelings, and thoughts. This chapter will discuss a variety of approaches and methods that can be utilized to improve children's social and emotional learning (SEL) and to encourage self-regulation.

Increasing Awareness of Social Issues

In social learning, social awareness serves as the basis. It entails being aware of and comprehending one's own feelings as well as the feelings of other people, in addition to having the ability to empathize with the viewpoints and experiences of other people. These are some methods that can be utilized to improve social awareness:

Teach youngsters to recognize and label a variety of emotions, both in themselves and in others. This is the first step in the emotional recognition process. Inspire children to communicate their feelings in a way that is beneficial to their health, and encourage conversations about feelings to become a normal part of their everyday lives.

When it comes to comprehending diverse points of view, it is important to guide youngsters in the process of perspective-taking by encouraging them to put themselves in the position of another person. Encourage youngsters to build empathy and understanding by having them participate in role-playing activities or by having them debate a variety of scenarios.

3. Active listening: Instruct youngsters on the significance of active listening in the process of establishing and maintaining healthy relationships. Encourage children to keep their attention on the person who is speaking, to keep eye contact, and to ask questions that will clarify the situation. Through the promotion of understanding and empathy, active listening leads to an increase in social awareness.

Developing Capabilities in Relationships

One's overall well-being and ability to self-regulate are both improved by having positive interactions. Here are some methods that can assist children in developing their relationship skills:

1. Communication Skills. Teach children excellent communication skills, such as listening, clearly expressing their thoughts and feelings, and resolving problems in a calm manner. In order to improve their communication skills, you should provide them with opportunity to practice and role-play different scenarios.

2. Cooperation and Collaboration: Provide children with opportunities to participate in group activities that require them to work together and cooperate. In order to tackle difficulties collectively, you should encourage them to collaborate, share duties, and work together. Through the promotion of teamwork and empathy, abilities in collaboration help to cultivate meaningful connections and promote self-regulation for individuals.

3. Fostering Empathy: Children can be assisted in the development of empathy by participation in activities that encourage understanding, compassion, and an attitude of kindness. They should be encouraged to consider how their actions affect other people and to have a conversation about how important it is to treat other people with respect.

4. Problem-Solving: In order to address conflicts or obstacles that take place in relationships, it is important to guide youngsters in the development of problem-solving skills. You should encourage them to come up with potential solutions, take into account the viewpoints of others, and look for outcomes that are beneficial to both parties. Self-regulation is improved through the development of problem-solving skills, which in turn promote successful decision-making and conflict resolution.

Taking Responsibility for One's Choices

The ability to make responsible decisions is a key component of both self-regulation and social and emotional learning (SEL). When making decisions, it is necessary to take into account ethical issues and to take into account the well-being of both oneself and other people. To encourage responsible decision-making, the following measures might be utilized:

Helping youngsters recognize their own personal values and comprehend the ways in which those values influence their decision-making is the first step in the value identification process. Inspire children to think about the potential repercussions that their actions could have, not only on themselves but also on other people.

2. Ethical Reasoning: Involve youngsters in conversations that investigate ethical conundrums and invite them to consider the various ways in which these problems could be resolved. Help them develop their ability to think critically and

urge them to consider the benefits and drawbacks of various courses of action.

Encourage children to learn strategies that will help them control their impulsive impulses and make decisions that are well thought out. I would like to encourage them to take a moment to pause, assess the situation, and think about several options before responding. Developing the ability to manage impulses helps improve one's ability to make appropriate decisions.

4. Helping children connect their decisions with their personal goals and values is the fourth step in the goal alignment process. It is important to encourage children to consider if the decisions they make are in line with their long-term well-being as well as the well-being of others.

Including Social and Emotional Learning in Everyday Life

In order for children to effectively benefit from social and emotional learning (SEL) for self-regulation, it is essential to include these activities into their day-to-day life. SEL can be promoted in a variety of settings using the following methods:

1. Classroom Integration: Include social and emotional learning activities in the regular routines of the classroom. You may start or end the day with a check-in on emotions, participate in activities that involve cooperative learning, and foster conversations on empathy and responsible decision-making while you do these things.

Home and Family: Inspire parents and other caregivers to implement social and emotional learning strategies in their homes. For the purpose of fostering open communication, empathy, and responsible decision-making, you should provide a setting that is trustworthy and encouraging. Involve the family in activities that will improve their social awareness as well as their ability to form relationships.

3. Community Engagement: Work together with the community in order to give chances for social and emotional learning. Investigate the possibility of forming collaborations with groups that centre their attention on social-emotional development and provide activities or programs that encourage self-regulation and overall well-being.

The fourth step is to model the behaviors that you wish to see in children and then reinforce those actions. During your interactions with them and other people, demonstrate empathy, active listening, responsible decision-making, and the ability to self-regulate. When children demonstrate skills related to social and emotional learning (SEL) and self-regulation, provide them with positive reinforcement and feedback.

We are able to cultivate a culture of self-regulation and develop lifelong skills that are essential to well-being and success by incorporating social and emotional learning (SEL) into the fabric of children's lives.

It may be concluded that social-emotional learning is an effective method for fostering self-regulation in youngsters. In order to equip children with the necessary skills to control their emotions, create meaningful connections, and make choices that are intelligent, we focus on boosting social awareness, building interpersonal skills, and fostering responsible decision-making. When we include social and emotional learning into our everyday lives, we are able to create an atmosphere that encourages children to self-regulate and promotes their general well-being.

The final chapter will be devoted to a contemplation of the transforming path towards self-regulation, as well as the provision of resources to sustain and continue this growth. Let us proceed together on this path of self-regulation, which will enable youngsters to realize their full potential and become the best versions of themselves.

6

Sustaining Self-Regulation: Reflection and Resources

I would want to offer my congratulations on taking the first step toward fostering self-regulation in children. As we get to the end of this book, it is vital to take stock of the significant progress that has been made and investigate the resources that can assist in maintaining and further improving self-regulation skills. The purpose of this final chapter is to ensure that you continue to empower children on their journey toward self-regulation by providing them with guidance and support.

Self-reflection and evaluation of oneself

Take a minute to think about the journey that has been taken up to this point. Take into consideration the development and achievements that you have seen displayed by the youngsters that you work with. Take some time to reflect on how you have developed as a teacher or caregiver in terms of assisting with self-regulation. In order to help you lead your reflection, here are some questions:

1. What new developments have you noticed in the children's ability to self-regulate their behavior?

2. What changes have you made to your approach to educating or providing care in order to better assist self-regulation?

3. What difficulties did you take on, and how did you find solutions to those difficulties?

4. Which strategies or methods have proven to be particularly effective in advancing the development of self-regulation habits?

5. In which aspects of self-regulation do you feel additional development or support is required?

Take advantage of this chance for personal and professional development by reflecting on your experiences. As you continue on this road, it is important to acknowledge the accomplishments you have achieved and to pinpoint areas in which you could make improvements.

Professional Development and Ongoing Education and Training Options

As an educator or caregiver, it is essential that you have a solid understanding of and the ability to self-regulate in order to provide support for children. For the purpose of expanding your knowledge in this field, you might want to think about participating in chances for professional development and continuing education. Take into consideration the following resources:

1. Workshops and Training: In educational contexts, it is important to look for workshops or training sessions that are centered on self-regulation opportunities. The chances presented here have the potential to offer children insights, practical solutions, and procedures that can help them better regulate themselves.

2. Courses Available Online: There is a plethora of courses available on the internet that cover themes such as self-regulation, social-emotional learning, and other relevant subjects. Investigate trustworthy online platforms that provide courses that may be completed at your own leisure or with the guidance of an instructor in order to enhance your knowledge and abilities.

Participate in professional groups and conferences: If you are interested in education, child development, or social-emotional learning, you should consider becoming a member of professional organizations. When you attend one of these organizations' conferences or events, you will have the opportunity to network with other professionals who share your interests and acquire insightful knowledge.

Staying up to speed on the most recent research and literature pertaining to self-regulation and social-emotional development is the fourth step in the literature review process. In order to broaden your knowledge and improve your profession, you should read journal articles, books, and other publications.

Collaboration as well as support from peers

Always keep in mind that you are not traveling alone on this path. Make connections with other professionals, caregivers, and educators who are interested in fostering self-regulation in children and who share your passion for this topic. When it comes to sharing ideas, methods, and best practices, it is important to engage in cooperation and peer support. Think about the following potential possibilities for working together:

1. Professional Learning Communities: Participate in or build a professional learning community that is centered on self-regulation. The purpose of these communities is to create a forum for people to work together, share resources, and talk about accomplishments and difficulties.

2. Participate in Online Forums and Social Media: Take part in online forums or social media groups that are devoted to education or social-emotional learning. Extending your network and gaining new insights can be accomplished by participating in conversations and exchanging ideas and information.

3. Regularly reflect on your own practice and seek input from coworkers or mentors. This is the third and last step in the reflective practice and feedback process. It is beneficial to one's professional development and one's ability to continuously improve to engage in reflective dialogue.

Collaboration Between Parents and Caregivers with

When it comes to maintaining children's self-regulation skills, it is absolutely necessary to work together with their parents and other caregivers. In order to assist self-regulation, it is important to cultivate open channels of communication and involve them as involved partners. The following is a list of strategies that lead to effective collaboration:

1. Your Parent or Caretaker Providing workshops or information sessions that are specifically geared toward parents and caregivers is a great idea. with

order to assist their child with self-regulating, parents should be provided with ideas and procedures that they can practice at home.

2. Newsletters and Resources: Make available on a regular basis newsletters or online resources that include advice, articles, and activities that are associated with exercises in self-regulation. You should encourage parents and other caregivers to investigate these materials and have conversations with their children about them.

3. Parent-Teacher Conferences: Make use of parent-teacher conferences as a chance to discuss the progress that a child has made in areas related to self-regulation. Collaborate on ways to provide the child with appropriate support, and share your views, strategies, and areas in which the youngster could improve.

It is important to keep in mind that the obligation of working together with parents and caregivers is a shared one. For the sake of the child, provide a setting that is encouraging and welcoming, one that encourages open communication and contributes to the development of a solid partnership.

Upholding a Mentality That Is Capable of Progress and Resilience

When embarking on this journey to encourage self-regulation, it is essential to keep a growth-oriented and resilient mindset from the beginning. In order to demonstrate resilience to the children you work with, you should view problems as chances for learning and embrace them. They should be guided in the development of a growth mentality, and they should be encouraged to consider failures as opportunities for personal development.

Create an environment that is supportive and encouraging, and be sure to acknowledge the development that each child has made and the efforts that they have put forth. Commemorate their achievements, regardless of how minor they may be, and emphasize the significance of tenacity, self-reflection, and an ongoing commitment to quality improvement.

Final Thoughts

In recognition of the critical role that self-regulation plays in children's academic achievement and overall well-being, we have traveled together in the process of fostering self-regulation in children. Children have been given the ability to effectively manage their emotions, thoughts, and behaviors as a result of our efforts to create an atmosphere that is conducive to learning, to build skills for self-regulation, to integrate social-emotional development, and to foster teamwork.

Keep in mind that the process of self-regulation is a journey that lasts a lifetime as you continue on this path of transformation. Maintaining a growth attitude, engaging in self-reflection, continuing your education, and working with others are all effective ways to sustain your personal growth. Seize the opportunity to leave a long-lasting impression on the lives of children by providing them with the tools they require to flourish in all aspects of their lives, including academics, social interactions, and emotional well-being.

Continue to motivate, encourage, and empower children as they make their way toward self-regulation, and be there to see the tremendous transformation that takes place in their life. The impact of your actions will be felt well beyond the pages of this book, and you are making a difference in the world.

I am grateful that you have chosen to accompany me on this journey of self-regulation. It is my hope that the work you do will continue to improve and enhance the lives of children.